Illustrated by Juliette Clarke
Words by Pam Brown and Helen Exley

Original edition published in 2011 by Helen Exley® LONDON in Great Britain.
This new edition published in 2021 by Helen Exley® LONDON in Great Britain.
Words by Pam Brown and Helen Exley © Helen Exley Creative Ltd 2011, 2021.
Illustrated by Juliette Clarke © Helen Exley Creative Ltd 2011, 2021.
Selection and arrangement by Helen Exley © Helen Exley Creative Ltd 2011, 2021.

ISBN: 978-1-84634-563-0

12 11 10 9 8 7 6 5 4 3 2 1

Helen Exley® LONDON
16 Chalk Hill, Watford, Hertfordshire, WD19 4BG, UK

January 1

A sister – even a sister you rarely see – is as much a part of your life as breathing.

All the words are by Pam Brown and Helen Exley © Helen Exley Creative Ltd 2021.

If you love this giftbook...
...you can find other HELEN EXLEY® gifts like it on
www.helenexley.com and
www.helenexleyusa.com

Helen Exley and her team have specialised in finding wonderful quotations for gifts of happiness, wisdom, calm and between families, friends and loved ones... A major part of Helen's work is to bring love and communication within families by finding and publishing the things people everywhere would like to say to the people they love.

Her books obviously strike a chord because they now appear in forty-five languages, and are distributed in more than eighty countries.

You can follow us on ⬛ and ⬛

January 2

Wherever you are,
you're never alone as long as you have a sister
on the planet.

January 3

The applause of a sister means far more
than that of any crowd.
For she sees your achievement.
She sees all that led up to it.

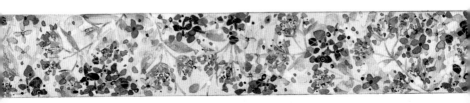

An only child faces the world alone.
You stand shoulder to shoulder
with your sister.

December 29

From our long acquaintance,
our close ties, our sharing
and our memories,
we have become so intertwined
that nothing can divide us.

January 5

Sometimes
you just need
a hand to hold –
and a sister
knows when.

December 28

A sister is a little bit of childhood
that can never be lost.

January 6

Nothing is ever
so frightening with
a sister
beside you.

December 27

We have known each other so long and so
well we are part of one another.
Our lives are interlocked.

January 7

Even the most loving sisters
regard the success of siblings
with a mixture of astonishment, delight,
and a degree of envy.

December 26

LIFE IS RICHER
WITH A SISTER.
THANK YOU
FOR IT ALL.

A sister can know
more about you
than anyone else on earth.

December 25

Dear Sister, stay young in heart forever,
Be what you have always been:
loving and kind and full of surprises.

January 9

No one chooses their sister –
so love and understanding,
patience and acceptance,
are learned little by little over
many years.

Keeping in touch
with you
is keeping in touch with
who I really am.

January 10

You may reshape yourself with time – but your sister knows who you really are.

December 23

Sisters disentangle problems in arithmetic and diet
and health. And when they're grown
they listen to your secrets, share your anxieties.
And never tell.

January 11

A SISTER IS A PORT IN ANY STORM.

December 22

You know who I really am – and accept me.
And forgive me. And yes! Are concerned for me.

January 12

What a beautiful place
the world is,
just because of you,
my loving sister.

December 21

Thank you for testing me
on my exam questions.
You are the kindest teacher.

January 13

A sister spends a great deal of her life
getting you into trouble –
and a great deal more in getting you out of it.

December 20

You know how to make me laugh.
You know my problems.
You understood me. You always have.

January 14

When something wonderful
has happened to you I light up with joy.

December 19

You are the person
I can't wait to talk to,
when I am alive and proud.
And also when my life
has crumbled
and I doubt myself.

January 15

Dear Sister.
Old friend. Old enemy.
Sharer of secrets.
Sharer of adventures.
Part of my life
forever and forever.

We know each other
as we always were.
We know each other's hearts.
We share our private
family jokes.
We remember family feuds
and secrets, family griefs
and joys.

January 16

We have no illusions about each other.
We know and can guess all the bad bits
but can go on caring. For life.

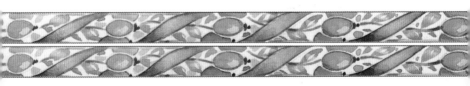

December 17

A sister is someone
who trusts you
to defend her.
Someone who thinks
you know the answers
to almost everything.

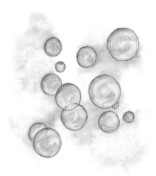

December *31*

A sister has shared many sorrows,
many fears, excitements, many joys.
A sister's life is entangled with one's own.
For always.

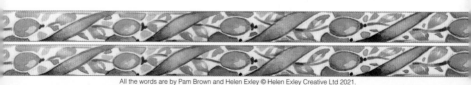

December 30

Ever since we were children
our joy has become more
wonderful,
our sorrows more bearable
because we shared them.
May it always be so.

January 17

We are involved in everything
the other does. We war at times – but
need each other, to be whole.

December 16

We are bound together by
a life of memories. Of laughter, squabbles,
tears and companionship.

January 18

With a sister in the house,
you can never get away with anything on the sly.

December 15

The world can never
be lonely while you are in it –
however far apart we are.

All the words are by Pam Brown and Helen Exley © Helen Exley Creative Ltd 2021.

January 19

Our friendship
is not based on the roles
of adulthood – but on
long, long acquaintance,
and deep
understanding.

December 14

Over our lifetimes
you have helped me
to find a solution or
an acceptance to almost
all my problems.

January 20

The best part of our lives
are the memories we share –
memories that come bubbling
to the surface at a word,
a gesture, an incident.

December 13

Time cannot change us.
We are bonded still.

January 21

World Politics was best illustrated by observing the two of us dividing our household chores.

However old
we become, however staid
and sensible –
something of us still roams
that far-off land of
childhood. Together.

January 22

Sisters are there to keep us human –
and they do.

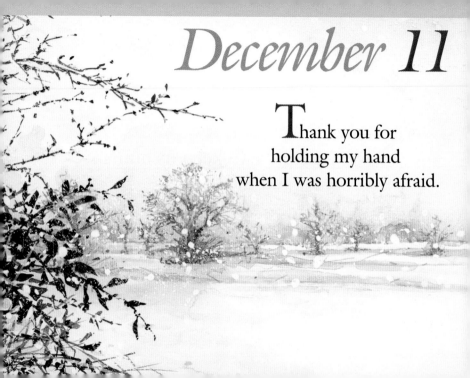

December 11

Thank you for
holding my hand
when I was horribly afraid.

January 23

We kick off our shoes,
unloosen belts and buttons,
raid the fridge,
sprawl by the fire
and talk and talk.
And talk.

A loving sister
carefully grows older
– and shares her time,
her strength,
her care with you.

January 24

Life without a sister
would have been far more lonely
– and far, far more dull.

December 9

Do you remember?
Those are the words that are the key
to all we mean to each other.

January 25

We discovered
very early
that forgiveness is
a necessity.

December 8

It's good to go out with friends
but, maybe best of all,
it's good to spend the day with a sister.
No need to impress – she'd only laugh.

January 26

I like it when I hear
old ladies talk about "Sister",
or "Brother".
It has become a title,
burnished by habit,
by affection until
it has the richness of
pure gold...

We go our separate ways,
but still a thread of silver links our lives.
Neither circumstance nor distance
can snap this slender filament.

January 27

Shared flu and sleepy
conversation in the quiet dark.
Berry expeditions.
Wading through drifts of leaves.
Shared silences.
Shared laughter. Together.

December 6

Siblings venture out
into the wider world
but never forget
that home called Family.

January 28

We never think we've aged or changed. To ourselves we are still eight years old – playing in the garden and sharing secrets.

December 5

When trouble comes,
brothers and sisters stand shoulder to shoulder.
They can take on the world.

January 29

We are linked together
by light, invisible chains –
stronger than steel
and indestructible.

December 4

Y‌ou get a frantic phone call
from your sister. You sigh.
But then you get out of the car and go
and rescue her.

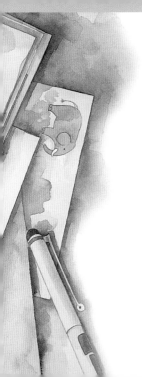

January 30

It doesn't matter if I don't
see you very often.
I'm busy. You're busy.
Just as long as I know
that you're there.

December 3

Sisters remember things
you would absolutely want to forget.
In graphic detail… With proof.

January 31

Anyone with a sister
is never short of total,
loyal support.

December 2

The deepest, saddest times in life
are when the support
and understanding of a sister
are most valued.

February 1

You, my oldest friend and enemy, companion, rival and collaborator.

December 1

We hold what's gone together.
We face what is to come together.

February 2

All the Firsts - do you remember?
You and I. Devouring every new discovery –
to enjoy later on, when we two were alone.

November 30

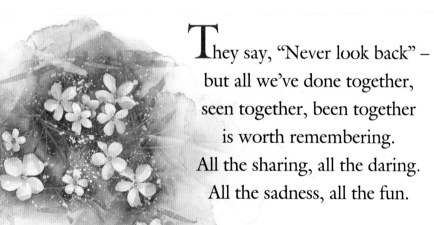

They say, "Never look back" –
but all we've done together,
seen together, been together
is worth remembering.
All the sharing, all the daring.
All the sadness, all the fun.

February 3

Every sister has a fund
of embarrassing stories she can bring out
at the most effective moment.

November 29

Do you remember whisperings
in the dark, the secrets,
the schemes, the giggling?
And quiet tears.
Paddings from bed to bed.

February 4

ANYONE WITHOUT A LOVING
SISTER COUNTS AS DEPRIVED.

November 28

A little bit of me is still nine years old,
building a snowman, skimming stones across the pond,
laughing with my sister on a windswept hill.

February 5

Sisters and brothers need not
love each other – or even like each other.
But they need each other.
Their roots are intertwined.

November 27

My second mother,
my first friend
– that's my sister.

February 6

ONLY WE REMEMBER
THE SMALL VICTORIES
AND SORROWS.

November 26

In a crisis we forget
differences and stand together.
When there isn't a crisis
we trust each other and enjoy
the years of contentment,
of quiet happiness and peace.

February 7

The gigglings in the dark,
the whispering of secrets,
the comfortings, the planning
of surprises...
It was a good beginning.

November 25

A sister is usually the only person
who will tell you the unvarnished truth.

February 8

It's a terrible thing being a second child.
The reason your mother is so delighted at your birth is
because you can wear all your elder sibling's hand-me-downs.

November 24

It's good to know that someone
is always on your side.

February 9

WITH A SISTER LIFE IS NEVER SHORT ON ASTONISHMENT.

November 23

We teach each other well.
That's because we share
some of the weaknesses
– and some of our main strenghts.
And because we are
on each other's side.

February 10

It's hard to be responsible, adult
and sensible all the time.
How good it is to have a sister whose
heart is as young as your own.

November 22

Thank you for all the last minute
repairs – the standing up stitchings,
the safety pin anchorings,
the painted over shoe scuffs.

Thank you for all the rescues,
all the cover-ups, all the scoldings
and comfortings.

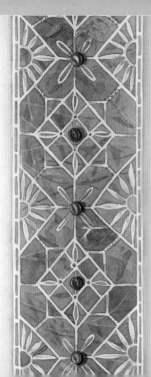

November 21

You raise your eyes to heaven
when I've got myself into
some most convoluted mess –
for you knew
where I was heading.

February 12

We will never, never grow old. Not in each other's eyes.

November 20

We may war
– but in times of trouble
immediately establish armistice,
and go to one another's aid.

February 13

Thank you for just being there.
Always.

November 19

Distance makes no difference to us, our lives have grown together.

February 14

A sister doesn't need
careful explanations.
She doesn't even
need full sentences...

November 18

Why is it that the perfect bag
for the perfect break is out with your sister
and her summer holiday?

February 15

I know that whatever the disaster I blunder into,
you will rescue me.
Pausing only to tell me what an idiot I've been.

November 17

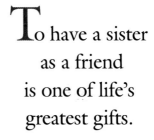

To have a sister
as a friend
is one of life's
greatest gifts.

February 16

When your sister blurts out
desperate apologies
and promises to replace whatever
it is – she's borrowed something
– and lost it!

You can rewrite the past,
but your sister
has the original manuscript.

February 17

Small siblings give you hugs
and sticky kisses
and cry if you are scolded,
and climb into your bed
when they are frightened,
and give you presents...
And teach you how to love.

No one knows us as we know
each other.
No one knows the whys and
wherefores of our lives as we do.
No one can so sympathize
with all we feel – in our victories,
our failures, our anxieties,
our hopes.

February 18

If you want an honest criticism, never ask a friend. Ask your sister. Though she's probably given you her frank opinion already.

November 14

Invariably – it's your sister who first finds out what you've been up to!

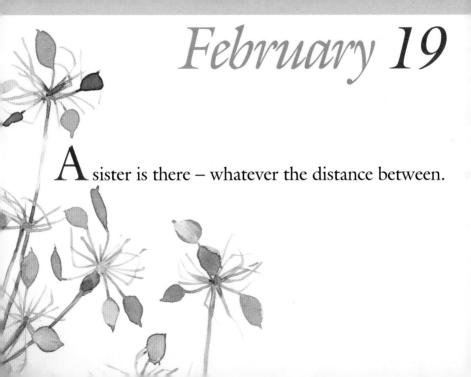

February 19

A sister is there – whatever the distance between.

November 13

A sister can calm
your fears
– because she knows
where they began.

February 20

Once our world was small enough
to understand, when you
and I were young.
Now often we feel ourselves lost
in its complexities.
But never totally – for each of us
is a landmark to the other.

November 12

We have a strange way of conversation,
you and I – and always have had,
ever since we first began to talk.

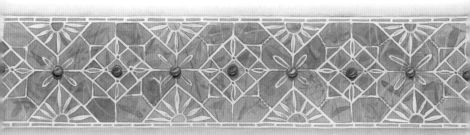

February 21

A sister is naggings and needlings,
whispers and whisperings.
Bribery. Thumpings. Borrowings.
Breakings. Welcomings home. Surprises.
Defendings and comfortings.
A sister is simply there.

After a small scolding,
you start to unravel it – telling me
that it isn't as bad as it looks.
Nothing is past repair.

February 22

How small we were.
How vulnerable.
And yet we had plans.
You and me together.

November 10

I<small>N TIMES OF TROUBLE,</small>
INNER WARS
ARE FORGOTTEN
AND SIBLINGS
STAND TOGETHER.

February 23

Sisters have the habit
of never quite forgiving sins
committed against them
at seven and a half.

November 9

However unalike we are,
our beginnings link us,
give us an understanding of each other
no one else can share.
You move through
my mind at ease among
my thoughts. Comfortable,
smiling, kind.

Older sisters
are always, always useful
– as a horse
– as a turner-of-ropes
– as a singer-to-sleep
– as a keeper-of-secrets.

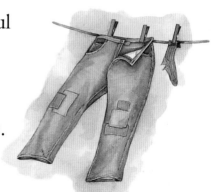

November 8

It's so good to have a sister
to worry about you
– and a sister to worry about.

February 25

A sister is someone
you can tell things
you'd not tell anyone else.
And who will let you
rant and rave and weep –
and make you cups of tea
when you're done.

When we talk about each other
– with affection or annoyance,
with anxiety or pride –
we speak almost exactly
as we did when
we were in our teens.

February **26**

The difference between a friend
and a sister is that with a sister the link
is indissoluble.

November 6

It's good to spend the day with a sister.
No need to impress – she'd only laugh.
No need to hide a stomach-ache,
a feeling of failure, a broken heart.
She takes you as you are.
Has a store of tissues and peppermints.
A listening ear.

February 27

Despite the differences, the rows,
the jealousies, we two know a unity
that no one else can understand.
We know so much about each other –
know the roots of every change.

November 5

Your partner is fine.
Your friends are fine.
But for the nitty-gritty stuff,
you need a sister.

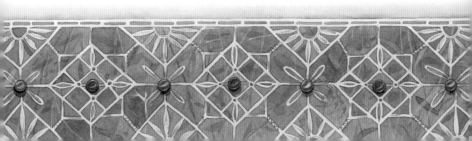

February 28/29

A SISTER IS VERY RARELY FOOLED.

November 4

A sister blames you for everything.
Still, a dead beetle in her bed evens things up!

March 1

Friendship is a splendid thing.
But it involves people who do not know
the family jokes, disasters, habits
and ridiculous adventures. You do.

November 3

A sister is invariably
the first to know when you have
decided to become
a vegan, a weightlifter,
a redhead.
When you are in love
or when you are deeply sad.

March 2

A sister has it in her power to kill
any tale stone dead
– by shouting out the ending!

November 2

A sister possesses
antennae that can
sense things that you
have borrowed!

March 3

Do you remember?
...And there we are,
five or six or seven
once again.

November 1

Friends come.
Friends go.
Sisters are forever.

How I pity people who haven't a sister.

October 31

SISTERS LISTEN
WHEN NO ONE ELSE
HAS THE TIME.

March 5

However much we disagree
I need your life to interlock with mine,
to know you share my secrets and my joys.
To know that you are there.

October 30

We are never completely surprised by anything that either of us does.

March 6

How strange that one child
should have a room
like a garbage tip
and the other a room like
a hospital surgery.

October 29

Friends came and went.
Studies, jobs and adventures.
Beliefs. Disasters. Ambitions.
But there has been a constancy. You, my sister.

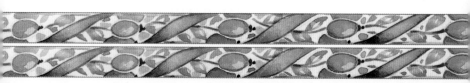

March 7

Memories,
both happy and sad,
hold us close and
always will.

October 28

When something wonderful happens,
first you phone your partner, then your mother –
and then your sister.
When something appalling happens –
you phone your sister.

Do you remember shuffling
about the kitchen in the dawn-light,
getting Dad's birthday breakfast?
The hushing and the clattering and the smell
of burning toast.

You cover for me. And keep schtum.

March 9

When a sister
on the phone says
"I just called for a chat..."
You know she hasn't!

October 26

Who else would endure my sillier moods
or forgive my more idiotic mistakes?
Only you. Why, I can't fathom.
But I give thanks that you do.

March 10

Friends get the slightly expurgated version
of your life.
Sisters know the original text.

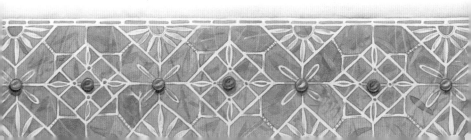

October 25

No one knows tumult
unless they have a sister getting ready
for the same event.

Sharing house chores
and a mother's love
teaches people about
compromise
and understanding.

October 24

You took my hand and led me along paths I would not have dared to explore alone.

March 12

An elderly respectable person gets together with a sister– and they go gleefully berserk.

October 23

So here you are.
Competent. Respected. Skilled.
And yet the sister who clambered out
along the oak tree bough and
waded in the racing river
and rode a tea tray down the hill.

March 13

We put our heads together
to Make Plans.

October 22

Differences
are totally set aside if a sister
is in trouble.

March 14

No matter how the world sees you –
your sister knows you as you really are.
And that is what keeps you human.

October 21

THANK YOU
FOR HAULING ME UP
WHEN I HIT
ROCK BOTTOM.

March 15

We share memories –
the wonder of nature,
the understanding of pain and
the beauty of love.

No one can get swollen-headed
if they have a sister.
She'll join in the applause –
but catch your eye, and wink.

Once we get together
we're inclined to drift
into the kitchen, slip off our shoes
– and talk.

October 19

A sister will get the muck off you
before anyone sees.
And she will keep quiet
when don't get the job you
hoped for. Total loyalty.

We persuade ourselves
we've learned a lot
from life, are wiser now;
but still a sister
smiles and nods
and sees us as we are.

October 18

It is a bitter thing to have a sister who takes a different size in shoes.

From earliest childhood
we staged wars over possessions.
"Mine. That's mine!
You've got my T-shirt on!"
Tennis shoes and gym bags.
Books. Games. Bikes.

October 17

The times you got far better marks
than mine, the times you got new shoes and I didn't.
…I envied you, your smile, your feet,
your sense of balance.
And it was years and years before I discovered
that you envied me.

March 19

A sister usually saw
your trouble coming.
Probably warned you.
She's disentangled you from
various catastrophes before.
Many, many times.

October 16

You're a sister. You praise me
– but then tell me
how to do it better.

All the words are by Pam Brown and Helen Exley © Helen Exley Creative Ltd 2021.

March 20

Who greets the news of your
most incredible achievement with,
"Good, I told you that you could do it."

October 15

Life without a sister would have been calmer
with far fewer hassles
– but without astonishments, plots and plans.
Without love.

March 21

A sister scolds you
when you're in any
sort of mess.
But bails you out.

A sister's pain is one's own pain.
Her joy, one's own...

A sister tries to get out of the front gate
before you notice that
she's wearing your new sneakers.

How can life ever be lonely
while we share the planet?

March 23

We're so interlocked with part of one another.
We've differed sometimes,
and a hint of sibling rivalry will always haunt us.
But the link is there forever.

October 12

Nothing a sister does
can completely astonish her sibling!

March 24

Sisters and brothers start out together
and though their paths divide
never forget their shared beginnings.

October 11

Thank you for hugging me
when all the world went wrong.

March 25

You only realize
how necessary a sister is
when you're
at the lowest point.

October 10

It's good to have a sister
to share your joys and fears.

March 26

SISTERS STAND BY
TO HELP PICK UP THE PIECES.

October 9

One learns the art
of sharing with a sister.
One has to.

March 27

You can be apart for years –
but suddenly there is an emergency
and hour-long phone calls –
advice given and advice taken.

October 8

In the woods,
I felt a hand
take mine –
and I knew
I could take on
any dragon
that I might meet.

March 28

The bond between us was
not made from flowers and loving sentiments
– but sitting on each other's heads,
arguing in whispers in the early hours.
From secrets.
From gigglings and raucous laughter.

October 7

You are my sister and dear friend forever.

March 29

In times of sadness
we hold each other
and share
and comfort.

Our lives are a tapestry of squabbles
and giggles, plots and adventures,
miseries and laughter.
Borrowings and gossipings and dreams.

March 30

Despite all distances
we are bound together.
Life long.

October 5

We know each other inside out,
upside down, bad and good,
with no acted roles, no disguises
and no secrets.
And so we like each other,
love each other, need each other.

March 31

Shared memories will link us forever.

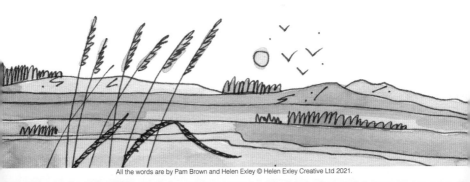

October 4

When there was excitement, an adventure, we shared it. Life alone would have been tidier and less fraught – but far, far more dull.

April 1

To lose all contact
with a sibling is to lose part
of one's being.

October 3

A sister tries never to say
"I told you so" –
but often can't resist.

We seem to grow closer with time
– the years are lit by acts of kindness
and by reminiscences.

A sister is loving,
helpful, kind.
But she never quite
forgot the time you
borrowed her charger –
and ruined it.

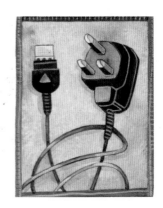

April 3

We've always seemed to have
a way of going into corners and
whispering
and giggling and hushing.

October 1

We have lived through
so much that nothing
could ever quite divide us.

April 4

Dear Friend.
Dear fellow buccaneer.
Dear Sister.

September 30

It's wonderful how
in an emergency
sisters simply ignore distance
and sort out your woes,
from afar.

April 5

We two have one beginning.
Our senses echoing the hushing of one heart.
We were gathered softly up,
nuzzled into safety.
Know the same scent and touch of love.

September 29

We have learned to accept
each other as we are.
Which is the most comforting feeling.

To have a sister
is to have an extra pair of eyes
an extra pair of ears
an extra pair of hands.
We show the world to one another.

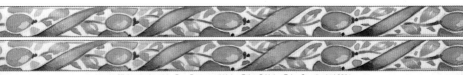

September 28

When you are a very old lady
in a wheelchair,
to me you will still be my little sister
laughing on the garden swing.

April 7

You may know that I've been a total idiot. But you always rescue me and then help to make me feel strong again. Thank you.

September 27

Teasings and arguments.
Amazing astonishments.
Rivalries and sharing.
Encouragement and comforting.
A shoulder to cry on.
You, my sister.

Someone to turn to.
Someone to keep secrets.
Someone to share delight,
excitement, sorrow.
Exasperating, puzzling
and surprising
– my best, my closest friend.

September 26

Thank you for doing what sisters do best –
ensuring my head stays the normal size, whatever
successes come my way.

April 9

When no one else understands, a sister does.

A little of our childhood joys and
sorrows stay forever and mark our lives.
Sisters remain always
something of what they were.

April 10

Sisters stand beside you
in your hour of triumph
and catch your eye and grin.

September 24

If I ran out of anything,
I could usually
find it in your bedroom.
Just so long as
you didn't catch me!

April 11

We can create
a secret world all to ourselves.

September 23

Growing up together, we shared each other's lives.

April 12

In times of trouble
any individual talent that either of us
has is shared.

Our lives are inextricably entwined.
When trouble comes all sibling rivalry
is forgotten and we give all our energies
to comfort, aid and rescue.

April 13

A sister with the same
measurements
is worth her weight in gold.

September 21

One may be a star,
a Chief Executive –
famous and rich and talented.
But one's sister
has the family photo album.
And a long memory.

April 14

A sister is a sister forever and ever.

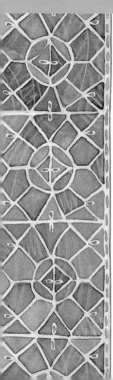

September 20

We are very old but still
just as much akin
as when they were very, very small.

April 15

We are grown and very
different now. People say –
"I would never have taken her
for your sister."
But we share the glimmering
dark, the deepest sorrow and loss
– and the safety of our
father's arms.

September 19

A sister doesn't need words.
She has perfected a language of smiles
and frowns and winks
– expressions of shocked disbelief.
You can undermine
any tale I'm telling.

April 16

We never forget the small adventures
we shared when we were little.

September 18

We planned the future
together – and so took
the first steps
in making it come true.

A home in which
siblings love each other
is a happy home.

September 17

When you win a competition, run a race, help an old person, I am the proudest person in the universe.

April 18

We do not choose our sisters
– they are wished on us.
But the blood-link often outweighs the element of
choice – and we need each other all our lives.

September 16

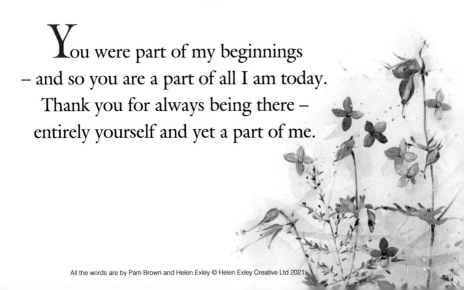

You were part of my beginnings
– and so you are a part of all I am today.
Thank you for always being there –
entirely yourself and yet a part of me.

April 19

A sister is the best person
to have with you
when you're shopping for clothes.
She tells you the truth.

All the words are by Pam Brown and Helen Exley © Helen Exley Creative Ltd 2021.

September 15

A sister's motto:
Help first.
Recriminations later.

April 20

"Do you remember?"
brings back those summer skies, the sweet,
high song of larks, the waist-high grasses.
The future charged with goals and targets.

September 14

You know
the real reason
why I do things.

April 21

Who can you call at three
in the morning,
stuck on the motorway,
marooned by snow,
covered in spots, jealous or jilted,
out on your ear,
nowhere to go? Your sister.

September 13

A sister knows all your faults –
but comes to the rescue
when you're in real trouble.

April 22

To have a sister
is to be involved in an ongoing
soap opera.

September 12

We may look old and wise
to the outside world.
But to each other, we are
innocent and vulnerable.

April 23

A sister exasperates.
A sister lets you down.
But she is your sister
and you wouldn't be
without her.

September 11

ONE NEEDS A SISTER
FOR A REALLY WILD
SHOPPING SPREE.

April 24

When we're standing together,
we make formidable opponents.

September 10

We argue over duties,
floor space, petty things, friends.
We fight until one of us
is in trouble –
then all arguments are
put on hold.

April 25

A sister is...
Someone to tell my secrets.
Someone to share my adventures.
Someone to stick up for me.
Someone to take care of.

September 9

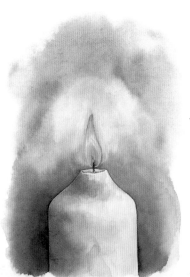

You can keep my secrets.
For life.

April 26

I need never call you in times of distress.
You are there in the blink of an eye.

September 8

L‌IFE IS NEVER DULL WITH A SISTER.

April 27

We fool this loud, polluted world,
you and I.
Our woods are deep and green and cool.
Our world is safe.
And we are young forever.

When friends
are not enough –
I'm glad
I can email you.

April 28

She's part of me
and I am part of her.
Until the ending of our days,
we will be part of
one another's lives.
However far apart, however
different, we are essential
to each other.

You don't interfere.
You just watch.
And then help pick up the pieces!

April 29

Thank you for warning me about the cold.
And not saying "I told you so"
when you were proved right.

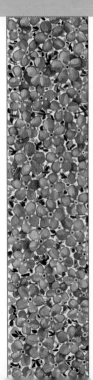

September 5

When we're out on a spree
all worries disappear,
and we are twenty years younger.

April 30

W HAT'S THE GOOD OF NEWS
IF YOU AND I
CAN'T SHARE IT?

September 4

Your joys are mine.
Mine yours.
What would I do
without you?
I would lose
half my life.

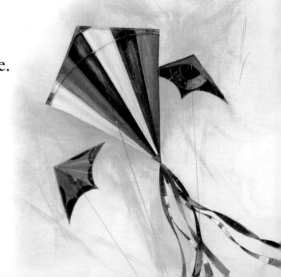

May 1

We bickered over little things.
We told tales, borrowed each other's
things without permission.
And yet – sided with one another
against authority.
Untangled homework.
Comforted each other.

All the words are by Pam Brown and Helen Exley © Helen Exley Creative Ltd 2021.

September 3

A sister stays at the same distance from us
in age as she has always done.
Until the very end of life she is given to advice
and exasperation.
Liable to say, "I told you so."

May 2

You and I will always worry about each other.

September 2

The eyes of siblings meet and exchange secrets. There is a fundamental understanding.

May 3

When you come through
the door, you have always hung up
all pretence with your coat.

September 1

We worry about each other quite a lot.
Can't be helped.
It's part of loving.

Having a sister, however far off,
makes the world less lonely.

How nice to have a sister to plot with.

May 5

I will donate a kidney.
Organize secret parties for you.
And lend you money.
I will praise, scold, rejoice and
weep for you
and stand by you forever.

August 30

A kind sister donates
her strawberries.
In return for unwanted
glacé cherries.

May 6

I wish I were a bit like you –
I always did.
I wish I could sing.
And could understand machines.
And make a decent omelette.
You feel the same?!
How very strange.

August 29

WITH A LOVING SISTER
BESIDE ME
I CAN STAND AGAINST
THE WORLD.

Sisters share the scent and smells
– the feel of a common childhood.
Hot raspberry jelly steaming in a bowl.
Dad's bright tie.
The pattern on the carpet.
We share a territory –
You and I.

August 28

We wander in and out of each other's lives –
interested, observant, helpful – sometimes exasperating.
But always strangely, as we used to be...
We never quite grow up.

A shared childhood
means a sea of wet suits,
books, oil paints, teddy bears,
make-up, posters, hockey sticks,
tennis rackets, half-eaten apples,
beads and bangles and
walking boots.

August 27

To have a loving sister
is to feel easy with existence.

When the river has changed course and is
running through the living room,
when one has bumped the car rather badly,
when one has a nasty and persistent pain...
a sister is simply there.

All the words are by Pam Brown and Helen Exley © Helen Exley Creative Ltd 2021.

August 26

Sisters are the people we practise on,
the people who teach us about fairness
and kindness and caring.

May 10

We know we can rely on each other
in the deepest of our problems. For life.

August 25

There is always a little ache
in your heart
for a sister who is far away.
You miss the secrets, the smiles...

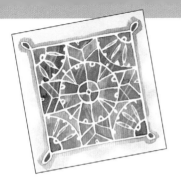

A little bit of every sister is still nine years old,
skimming stones across the pond,
laughing with her sibling on a windswept hill.
They have a secret and are forever young.

August 24

You are a friend
and a defender – a listener,
a counsellor, a sharer of delights.
And sorrows too.

May 12

We have done some very stupid things, you and I.
And yet we've learned over the years
patience and understanding,
loss and forgiveness.

August 23

We look at one another,
bemused to find
so many years have passed.
And that we've come
to wear so baffling a disguise.

Sisters and brothers working together
can achieve amazing things.

August 22

Thank you for being the sort of sister
everyone should have – a companion
in adventure, a sharer of secrets,
a loyal supporter. A friend.

May 14

There is a country
that we share that is our own –
books and adventures,
holidays, astonishments,
loves and cats and hopes.
A place where we can go together
and leave the years behind.

I look forward to being with you,
just to tell good news,
a joke, an adventure, an astonishment.

May 15

A sister has no delusions.
She lived with you too long. And so, when you achieve
some victory, friends are delighted –
your sister holds you in silence and shines
with happiness. For she knows the cost.

August 20

Even the most dignified of people
are inclined to baffle outsiders
when they're with their sister.
They share a world of private
memories – and jokes.
And are inclined to giggle.

All the words are by Pam Brown and Helen Exley © Helen Exley Creative Ltd 2021.

Horw very lonely the world would seem
if one didn't know one's sister was around somewhere.

August 19

You sigh and get down to sorting out the mess into which I have dug myself.

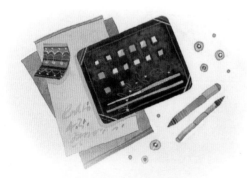

May 17

Thank you for reading to me when I was ill.
Thank you for blowing my nose
when I was very small.
Thank you for taking care of me.

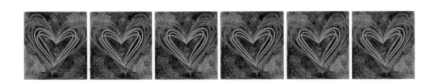

For teaching me to swim.
For driving away
the bogeymen.
For being my friend
when no one else seemed to be.
Thank you.

May 18

One's sister vaguely believes
that what is yours is hers.

August 17

Odd how you were wearing socks
exactly like the new pair
in my sock drawer!

May 19

You know my roots.
You know my weaknesses
and the blind spots.
And, mercifully,
you know my best bits.

August 16

There's Mother's Day and Father's Day.
There should be a Brother's
and a Sister's Day.

May 20

A sister reminiscing
about the past uses the same
book reference as oneself.

August 15

A shared and happy childhood gave us a place of safety all our lives.

Anyone with a sister
is one up on everyone else
in social survival.

August 14

For all the times you cleaned me up before Dad saw me. For helping me remember that awful nine times table. For punching Herbert Johnson on the nose. For sewing on my missing buttons. Thank You!

May 22

When you need to help or
protect your sister,
you suddenly feel stonger,
older, wiser.
And you love her with all
your heart!

Our greatest treat
was to sleep on a mattress
on the floor of
each other's bedroom.
And talk ourselves
to sleep.

May 23

Sisters teach you to be human.

Sisters remember –
A great deal too much!

It's your sister who said,
"Remember the last five times you felt like this"
– and hauled you home until
you found your senses.

August 11

If you dare not wake your parents or your friends –
you call your sister.
You may have to pay for it by being nagged
all the way home – but she'll get you there.

How useful it is
when a sister is gifted
in different areas
of the curriculum!

August 10

How good it is
to have someone
who accepts me as I am.
A sister's love
is never blind.

May 26

No need to hide a sniffle,
a stomach-ache, a broken heart.
Your sister takes you as you are.
Has a store of tissues.
A listening ear. Sympathy.

August 9

Your past is the same territory
as mine.
We both know every path, every stream,
every turn in the road.

Sisters know when to yell at you –
and when to hug.

August 8

N o one is ever going to watch
every single thing you do
with such absolute rapture as a sister.

All the words are by Pam Brown and Helen Exley © Helen Exley Creative Ltd 2021.

May 28

I often feel you are always there in me
as a way of making sense of the new experiences.
I'll think, "Oh you would love this"
or I send you a message.

August 7

When you can't tell your mother for fear
she'll have a heart attack,
that's the time you need a sister
– who will say "I told you so".
And then get on with unravelling you.

We are grown now,
but still I hear your voice in memory.
"Stand up for yourself." "Think!"
"Sleep on it."
"Cheer up, be brave,
I'm right behind you."
And you are. Always.

August 6

You are liable to nag.
To refuse to lend me things. To scold.
But you also disentangle problems in arithmetic.
You share my secrets, listen to my anxieties.
And never tell.

We are bound together by a thread.
Invisible, sometimes forgotten, but unbreakable.

August 5

I can never
be utterly lonely, knowing
you share the planet.

Everyone needs a sister
for advice.
Everyone needs sisters
to give them foolproof recipes.
To exchange information.
To listen.

August 4

What would I do without you? You know all my fears and weaknesses, all my secret hopes and dreams. You share my memories.

June 1

A pot of tea,
quiet music and
memories of childhood.
Shoes off.
THE HAPPY HOUR.

August 3

A sister is there when you're in trouble.
She tells you to comb your hair, corrects your work
and supports you in deepest sorrow.

June 2

Some time or other
we need a sister badly
– and you will be there.
If ever you can!

August 2

Sisters take up things.
Yoga. Clay pigeon shooting.
Saving the planet.
Flower arranging.
Good Works.
Painting in acrylic.

June 3

We learned about life together, you and I.
Dealt with disappointments, failures, loss.
Shared joy in victories and in astonishments.
Scolded and comforted. Plotted and planned.
And we've come through – and smile
at one another as old friends.

August 1

Y ou've infuriated me, exasperated me,
wearied me all my life long – yet if you're
silent just for a week, I find some excuse
to call – worried to death
that something might be wrong!

W̶hat is the pleasure
in passing your finals
if you have not got a sister
to hug?

July 31

Sisters! They annoy, interfere, criticize.
Indulge in monumental sulks,
in huffs, in snide remarks. Borrow. Break.
Monopolize the bathroom.
Are always underfoot.

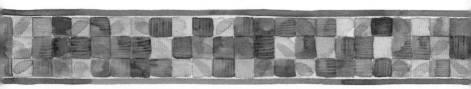

June 5

I need you to boost my morale
when I have decided
that I'm no use at anything.

July 30

I think of you so much. Think of me a little. And phone!

June 6

Cleaning a home
shared by a sister is
like a major archaeological dig
– possessions dated by strata.

July 29

We need to keep in touch
– for, like it or lump it,
we are part of one another.

June 7

A SISTER CAN GIVE COMFORT
IN EVERY DISMAL CIRCUMSTANCE.

Sometimes, just sometimes,
other people just won't do.
You need your sister.
To talk. To wander round
the garden.
To rediscover time that's past.

June 8

We have something no one in our lives can share –
those years of childhood with their hopes and terrors,
their secrets and their plans.
Only we know what made us as we are today...

July 27

Together we can get
into tricky situations.
Together we can get ourselves
out of them.

June 9

Our heroine said
it was wonderful.
My best friend said it was incredible.
You said it was rubbish.
And you were right.
So I'll do it again.
Better this time.

All the words are by Pam Brown and Helen Exley © Helen Exley Creative Ltd 2021.

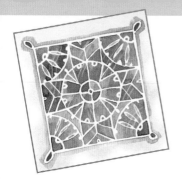

July 26

A sister is a sure preventative of a swollen head.
At the first sign of smugness or superiority she applies
a bucket of icy water – guaranteed to shrink
the sibling's head to its proper size!

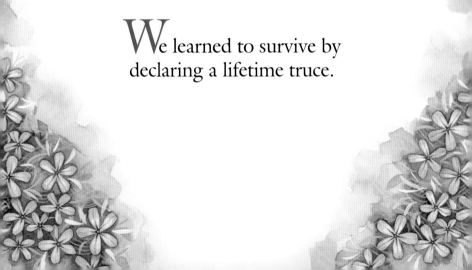

June 10

We learned to survive by declaring a lifetime truce.

July 25

Thank you for all the things you've lent me.
Thank you for all the things you've sent me,
made for me, shown me how to do.

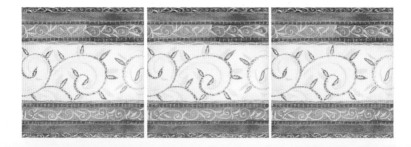

June 11

We love to make a plan.
It could be a small thing, like a surprise
for one of our children or it could be working
together to make sure our parents
are nursed and cared for.

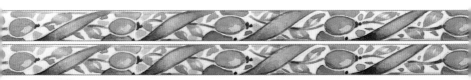

Grown-up sisters
still have this built-in
instinct to blow your nose
and pull up your socks.

June 12

At the first sign of incipient smugness
or superiority
sisters douse you in cold water
– and shrink you back to your proper size.

July 23

When I didn't want to worry our mother
– I worried you.
Thanks.
From me.

June 13

Other people we know
a little or a lot...
as much as they reveal,
as much as we discover.
Only siblings know each other
as they really are.

July 22

When my whole world had fallen in, thank you for holding my hand when I was horribly afraid. Thank you for taking care of me.

June 14

Distance
IS ELASTIC
WHEN IT COMES TO
BROTHERS AND
SISTERS.

July 21

In times of trouble, a sister scolds –
but rescues you.
And grins. And makes a cup of tea.

Dear Sister,
Stay young in heart forever.
Be what you have always been.
Loving and kind
and full of surprises.

July 20

We are strangely linked.
Our bond is invisible, intangible, strong.
We know the hows and whys of each another.

Sisters man the battlements
of the same castle
and keep it secure against harm.

July 19

For we have shared so much,
understood each other so well,
that two words will summon up a history,
an incident, a time of wild excitement.
Half a sentence can plunge us into laughter –
to the utter bewilderment of strangers.

June 17

There is something special
about walking up the road
with your sister beside you,
safe and secure and confident.

July 18

A mother's birthday
requires our total co-operation.
A great deal of whispering.
Careful budgeting.
Long talks, remembering
a lifetime of her care and love.

June 18

You have a way of forgetting what you did with my T-shirt but remember exactly how long I've had your laptop...

July 17

Let disaster strike – and you
come roaring to the rescue.
Heaven help the so-and-so who's
caused the misery!

June 19

You know me as I am.
Not as I appear to be.
Not as I attempt to be.
But as I really am.

You... someone to take care of.
Someone who will be there
in times of fear or
sickness and in times of joy.

All the words are by Pam Brown and Helen Exley © Helen Exley Creative Ltd 2021.

June 20

A sister's past is the same territory
as one's own.
So we can always start midway
through any story.

July 15

Dear Sister. You've never actually
lied to save my skin.
But you've tidied up the truth...
Thank you!

June 21

You'll not waste time with words –
but get down to the practicalities.
Which may entail a bed
for the night, a loan, a doctor,
a lawyer. Or simply some
shrewd and uncomfortable advice.

All the words are by Pam Brown and Helen Exley © Helen Exley Creative Ltd 2021.

July 14

We rejoice
in each other's success.
Better than anyone,
we know the struggles
by which it was earned.

June 22

A corner of one's mind
is always set aside
for one's sister.

July 13

A devoted
sister makes you feel
ten feet tall.

June 23

We share one mother
and so share a small, safe world.

July 12

We share sorrows
that no one can understand.
We share joys that are our secret treasure.
Our lives are bound together.

June 24

You stood on the sidelines of my life –
and sometimes you yelled very loudly.

No one praises sisters
or writes songs about them.
Sisters are simply there –
like your right arm.

Distance doesn't matter.
If you can't be with me when things go pear-shaped
you know me well enough
to tell me how to put things right.

July 10

There will be greater loves –
but none so deeply rooted
as that between siblings.

June 26

Sisters are different.
They heard about your problems.
They lived through all your
triumphs, all your disasters,
all your loves and losses.

July 9

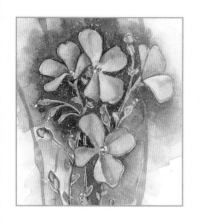

*S*ometimes a sisterly cuddle is what you are looking for.

June 27

We've come a long way together –
and shared the hardships
and the happiness
we've met along the road.
You are the best of company.

You smile when I tell one of my stories – because you know where the decoration has been added.

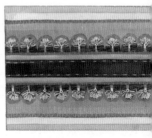

June 28

The world grows old.
But we hold
the springtime
of our lives
forever bright and young.

Siblings learn to accept people
as they are – not as they want them to be.
They are the training ground
for dealing with the human race.

Alone, the past is a shifting,
uncertain memory – but, having a sister
who shared those years, we have assurance.
Alone, it is but half remembered.

A sister understands you
better than a partner or a lover ever will.
They've known you from the very start.
In detail.

We have shared so much
we are a part of one another.

July 5

When the sky fell in,
you were there.
You gave me strength and
saw me through.

Your writing on the envelope,
your voice on the phone – and at once I am alert:
"What's happened? What has she done?
Where is she going?"

July 4

Sisters know too much
about your past. And they have memories
like elephants.

July 2

A sister knows all your faults and blemishes. In detail. So you never have to cook up excuses or assume disguises.

We disagree all the time.
Remember things quite differently.
Disapprove of one another's choices.
Are maddened by each other's habits.
But we are necessary
in some strange way
to each other's existence.